QUANTUM PEARLS
Finding Spiritual Wisdom in the Mundane Moments

(noun) **Quantum:** discrete quantity of energy, a share or portion

(noun) **Pearls:** person or thing of great <u>rarity</u> and worth; **wisdom, luck, purity, and love**. Like other precious stones and crystals, they contain powerful energy and abilities. That is why some believe pearls have the power to heal the body, mind, and soul.

(noun) **Quantum Pearls: dense bits** of **wisdom and spiritual energy** that can be found buried deep in the mundane moments of ordinary everyday life.

QUANTUM PEARLS

Finding Spiritual Wisdom in the Mundane Moments

Christopher M. Jones, Ph.D.

Published by Truth Publications, LLC
www.truth-brand.com

Quantum Pearls™
ISBN: 978-1-7366112-9-6
Copyright © 2023 by Jones Squared Productions

To my jewel of the Nile. Jerrilyn, thank you for helping me find the deeply buried quantum pearls of life.

Why Quantum Pearls

L ife can often feel routine, fast-paced, stressful, and common; much like a hamster wheel. Unlike that wheel, however, even the most mundane life is filled with spiritual wisdom. I call this spiritual wisdom, *Quantum Pearls*™. Quantum pearls are often buried deep, in plain sight, and I believe that our task is to excavate our daily lives to find these valuable pearls. I have done close examinations of many of my mundane, random, daily experiences and uncovered quantum pearls that I'm sharing in this 30-day devotional.

The pearls in this devotional were extracted during my time in Boston, Massachusetts. I led the young professionals at Morning Star Baptist Church – where I met my beautiful wife – and would always look for ways to encourage the group. Sunday service would leave us focused and charged, but it was clear that life was extremely busy for everyone, and by midweek, we were all hungry for more spiritual nourishment. We all wanted some way to feed our midweek spiritual hunger. To help address our collective hunger, I started regularly sharing ways that I had re-examined my daily experiences and found bits of spiritual wisdom, quantum pearls, buried right under my nose. These notes were a blessing when I first shared them and my prayer is that by reading and reflecting on quantum pearls, you will not only enjoy insights that I have gained, but you will also learn how to extract quantum pearls from the mundane activities of your own life.

This devotional is meant to provide just the right boost for those navigating life's journey and seeking to do it within God's will. This devotional is written for those seeking valuable pearls (like the merchant in Matthew 13:45-46). *Quantum Pearls* is also for those looking to build the muscle of finding pearls buried in their own daily activities. Quantum is a term for a discrete quantity of energy or a required amount. Pearls are things of great worth, wisdom, purity, and love. Together, Quantum Pearls contain powerful energy and abilities, and have the power to help heal the body, mind, and soul. Our job is to seek and find quantum pearls in our lives. This devotional helps us do just that.

Quantum Pearls is for anyone looking to see their routine, fast-paced, stressful, and common life in a whole new light!

Table of Contents

BURN BABY BURN!

Original Date: 06/08/2005

Passage: James 1:26-27

26 If anyone considers himself religious and yet does not keep a tight rein on his tongue, he deceives himself and his religion is worthless. 27 Religion that God our Father accepts as pure and faultless is this: to look after orphans and widows in their distress and to keep oneself from being polluted by the world.

There is a company in the South that disposes of low-level radioactive material. This company does not deal with nuclear power plant fuel (which is high-level radioactive material). It disposes of materials like the clothes people wear when they go in for radiation therapy or the actual machines used to transport nuclear fuel.

Recently, this company decided to build an additional type of disposal device. This new disposal device would essentially burn the material down to ashes, and the ash would then be compacted and sent away to be recycled.

Even though the company had received all the necessary government approval it needed to build the incinerator, the company still could not proceed. Various community groups were up in arms and were halting the project.

These community groups were upset because they strongly believed that burning radioactive material would cause radiation to seep into their groundwater. They also believed that it would cause airborne radiation to get into their systems. Even though the company already had all the necessary government approvals, there was a chance that these community groups would stop this project from moving forward.

The community said, "NO WAY, NOT IN MY NEIGHBORHOOD!" There is no guarantee that this project would cause pollution; it *might* cause pollution, but there is no guarantee that it actually *would.* Yet, these community organizations believed that *might* was enough to say, "NO WAY."

Imagine if we had the same "NO WAY" reaction to things that might pollute our communities, our churches, our families, and us. Not to mention the things that *DO* pollute our churches, our communities, our families, and each of us.

What things *might* cause pollution in your life?

_____

_____

_____

_____

What are ways that you can stop this pollution before it even

has a chance to move forward?

_____

_____

_____

_____

_____

CLOSELY SEPARATED

Original date: 03/30/2005

Passage: Isaiah 59:1-3

[1]Surely the arm of the LORD is not too short to save, nor his ear too dull to hear. [2]But your iniquities have separated you from your God; your sins have hidden his face from you, so that he will not hear. [3]For your hands are stained with blood, your fingers with guilt. Your lips have spoken lies, and your tongue mutters wicked things.

Two students of mine found themselves in a unique situation. They are both college students at the Massachusetts Institute of Technology (MIT) and were dating. Both had gotten accepted into the top graduate schools on the east and west coast (MIT, the University of California at Berkeley, and Stanford).

The problem was that the young man really wanted to stay at MIT for graduate school and the young lady really wanted to go to California for graduate school. For a young relationship, this can be a very scary development.

The young lady came to me asking for advice. After talking for a while, I realized that neither one would really be happy if they gave up their dreams. This unhappiness would only cause resentment and create significant barriers in their relationship. I ultimately suggested to them that it is better to be "separated geographically" and "close emotionally" than to be "close geographically" and "separated emotionally".

This discussion reminded me that there are thousands of couples in relationships who are miserable because they don't talk, don't listen, and don't share with each other. The primary explanation for these failures in open communication with each other is because one (or both) of them carry severe resentment towards the other for any number of reasons. This situation proves the saying that "the loneliest place on earth can be in a marriage."

Unfortunately, this is often the case in our relationship with God. He is so close, yet we are so separated from Him.

One of the things I am working to do is examine the relationships that are important to me and determine if I am doing anything that might cause or contribute to separation. Do I have resentment or frustration? Are my needs being ignored or do I feel that they are being ignored? Am I doing (or not doing) anything that might cause resentment or frustration on the part of the other person in the relationship? Am I ignoring the needs of the other person, or do they feel that I'm ignoring their needs?

These are the questions I am asking...and it starts with my relationship with God!! Note: Of course, with God, it is definitely my sins (ignoring Him, being a spoiled brat) that cause the separation.

When do you feel close to God?

_____

_____

_____

_____

_____

_____

What are three things you get from this closeness to God?

_____

_____

_____

What are three things that keep you
from this closeness to God?

_____

_____

_____

What will you do today to maintain
your closeness to God?

_____

_____

_____

_____

CONTINUOUS PRODUCTION

Original date: 07/13/2005

Passage: Jeremiah 17:7-8

⁷But blessed is the man who trusts in the LORD, whose confidence is in him. ⁸He will be like a tree planted by the water that sends out its roots by the stream. It does not fear when heat comes. its leaves are always green. It has no worries in a year of drought and never fails to bear fruit.

As we navigate our busy lives, as we solve problems, as we overcome obstacles, we occasionally have moments of victory. Many of us, in our moments of victory, think about how we might help someone else. This is great. I think about the student who does well in a class and then is willing to tutor others. I think about the pro football player who gives back to his community. I think about the lottery winner who pays her family's debts. I think about the married couple, living happily together, who takes time to minister to other couples. During these moments of victory, we often bear much fruit.

But, what about the student who fails the test? What about the football player who didn't make the team and is financially broke? What about those individuals who are deep in debt themselves? What about the married couple forced to live miles apart? How much fruit do they bear?

We have this tendency to become very self-centered when things don't go our way. Imagine a world where we always not only thought about loving and caring for others but actually did love and care for others -- even when we think no one loves or cares for us. Imagine a world where we gave to others all the time, even when we felt as if we had nothing left to give. Imagine a world where we NEVER FAILED to bear fruit and, instead, we were continuous producers of fruit. That's the world God wants! A world of continuous production!

What gift(s) do you have that you can give to others regardless of your own life situation?

_____

_____

_____

_____

What two things can you do today to produce and share fruit?

_____

_____

_____

_____

COUNT THE COSTS

Original date: 07/13/2007

Passage: Proverbs 20:25

25It is a trap for a man to dedicate something rashly and only later to consider his vows.

Have you ever been overwhelmed? Have you ever asked yourself, "I wish I had just one day to sit and rest?" Have you ever wondered why your bank account was so low and felt as though there is always something (or someone) else to pay?

There was a time when I would consistently find myself overwhelmed. I have had to run from one commitment to the next, drop the clothes off at the cleaners, dash over to a meeting, leave for a quick haircut, dash off to another meeting, stop by the post office on the way, finish the paper while on the bus headed to a reception, get home by 4pm to meet the delivery truck, change for a dinner meeting, get home to review emails that have been piling up and read a stack of papers to prep for the next day. I was completely out of my mind. To be totally open and honest, I still often find myself in the same situations. Even now, I often find myself with much more work to be done, due to commitments, than I have time to complete.

There was also a time when I would consistently find myself with "more month at the end of my money." I would pay all my bills and promise that the next few months were going to be different. In the next few months, I wasn't going to let my bank account see negatives. Looking back, I see that much of my money went to good things. I would give a nice offering (above tithes) in church. I would take friends out to eat. I would support the local charity. I would pay for books or supplies others needed. I would send money to relatives, only to find that the amount I sent them was more than what I needed to cover a bill I had forgotten to pay. I would even allow relatives to use my credit (since theirs was horrible), only to find that the accounts had gone unpaid and ended up being charged off.

So, what was the problem? Most of those things were positive and sprang from good intentions. Most of those things were relatively important matters. Most of them were directly helping others. The problem was... I did not count the costs before committing!

Had I counted the costs before committing, I would have realized that I needed to include travel time between tasks. I would have accounted for the fact that meetings run long, and traffic gets jammed. I would have realized that to do a great job on a proposal I needed to sit and focus.

Had I counted the costs before committing, I would have realized that I could not eat out all the time and I certainly could not pay for others. Had I counted the costs, I would have realized that if I could not cover my bills for the next few months, then I should not pay for books and supplies for others. Had I counted the costs, I would have realized that money "loaned" was often money "lost." Had I counted the costs, I would have realized that I could not trust others to take care of my credit as I would. Had I just counted the costs? Be sure to count the costs...before you commit!

What are three areas where you should have counted the costs
before committing, but you did not?

_____

_____

_____

What decision(s) are you making today where you could pause
and count the cost before committing?

_____

_____

_____

Day 5

DRY SPELL

Original date: 06/15/2005

Passage: *My Utmost for His Highest*

Recently, I've been experiencing a serious dry spell. Typically, I can look around and am inspired by the air, the grass, cars, planes, you name it and I get inspiration. Unfortunately, in the past few days, no matter where I look, I'm not inspired. I seem to be at a loss for what to share.

While doing devotion this morning, I read *My Utmost For His Highest* by Oswald Chambers and felt that his comments were very timely. They really blessed me, so I've decided to share his thoughts today.

Devotional: (from Oswald Chambers' *My Utmost for His Highest* based on II Peter 1:5)

> You have inherited the Divine nature, says Peter (v4), now screw your attention down and form habits, give diligence, concentrate. "Add" means all that character means. No man is born either naturally or supernaturally with character, he has to make

character. Nor are we born with habits; we have to form habits on the basis of the new life God has put into us. We are not meant to be illuminated versions, but the common stuff of ordinary life exhibiting the marvel of the grace of God. Drudgery is the touchstone of character. The great hindrance in spiritual life is that we will look for big things to do. "Jesus took a towel...and began to wash the disciples' feet."

There are times when there is no illumination and no thrill, but just the daily round, the common task. Routine is God's way of saving us between our times of inspiration. Do not expect God always to give you His thrilling minutes but learn to live in the domain of drudgery by the power of God.

It is the "adding" that is difficult. We say we do not expect God to carry us to heaven on flowery beds of ease, and yet we act as if we did! The tiniest detail in which I obey has all the omnipotent power of the grace of God behind it. If I do my duty, not for duty's sake, but because I believe God is engineering my circumstances, then at the very point of my obedience the whole superb grace of God is mine through the Atonement.

What is your routine when you are in the domain of drudgery?

What can you do to "add" character during this drudgery?

JUICY FRIED CHICKEN BREAST

Original date: 08/19/2004

Passage: Matthew 25: 41-46

41 "Then he will say to those on his left, 'Depart from me, you who are cursed, into the eternal fire prepared for the devil and his angels. 42For I was hungry, and you gave me nothing to eat, I was thirsty, and you gave me nothing to drink, 43I was a stranger and you did not invite me in, I needed clothes and you did not clothe me, I was sick and in prison and you did not look after me.' 44 "They also will answer, 'Lord, when did we see you hungry or thirsty or a stranger or needing clothes or sick or in prison, and did not help you?' 45 "He will reply, 'I tell you the truth, whatever you did not do for one of the least of these, you did not do for me.' 46 "Then they will go away to eternal punishment, but the righteous to eternal life."

The other day, Jerrilyn and I decided to eat at what might be my favorite Boston restaurant—Chef Lee's. If you've never had Chef Lee's, you are really missing out. For someone like me who was raised on great southern cooking, Chef Lee's is heaven.

When we got there, we both decided to order the fried chicken dinner. I ordered mine with macaroni and candied yams. Jerrilyn had hers with macaroni and collard greens. There was more than sufficient chicken for our order; however, they had just brought out a new batch of legs and thighs (which Jerrilyn loves) and it would be another 15 minutes before they brought out more breasts. You better believe I was going to wait.

We took our seats, and I faced the window, enjoying macaroni, yams, and my beautiful wife. I thought to myself "Life is good and is going to be even better when I get that juicy fried chicken breast—hot out of the kitchen."

Twenty minutes later, my chicken was ready. It was worth every minute of the wait time. Jerrilyn and I were having a wonderful conversation, laughing, and joking. I was enjoying the best chicken I'd had in a while…now life was truly great!

Halfway through eating my chicken (which I cleaned to the bone, of course), I noticed someone standing by the window. He looked at me, trying to get my attention. I wasn't sure what he was saying, but I assumed he wanted money or food. "I wish he would move along and leave me alone," was the thought going through my mind. So, I put my head down and waited for him to leave. He left and I enjoyed the rest of my meal…and boy was it good.

Shortly before we left the restaurant (headed to church like the good Christians we were), I got a stabbing pain in my heart and my soul dropped. What if I had just ignored an angel? What if I had just ignored Jesus? Even worse, I had just ignored a brother! God forgive me!!

What is grabbing so much of your attention that you could miss an angel?

_____

_____

_____

How can you make space, today, to ensure you don't ignore a brother?

_____

_____

_____

_____

GRADUATION TIME

Original date: 06/22/2005

Passage: I Corinthians 3:12-14

[12]If any man builds on this foundation using gold, silver, costly stones, wood, hay or straw, [13]his work will be shown for what it is, because the Day will bring it to light. It will be revealed with fire, and the fire will test the quality of each man's work. [14]If what he has built survives, he will receive his reward.

May and June are always exciting times! There's pomp and circumstance in the air. Families are gathering. The atmosphere is filled with a sense of completion and accomplishment. Students of all ages are reaping the benefits of their years of effort. It's graduation time!!!

This time reminds us that study and hard work have been tested. Those who graduate have passed the test. Whatever that test may be. For some, it's completing a dissertation. For some, it's an exit exam. For others, it's passing all their classes with a certain grade. Either way, there was a test and the graduates passed it.

Their reward is twofold: receiving recognition for success in passing the test and being allowed to move to the next phase in life where there will undoubtedly be more tests.

Have we passed the tests that God has designed for our life? Can He recognize us for our success? Are we ready to receive our reward? More importantly, if we do receive our reward, do we understand that more tests are on the way?

Let's work so that our work survives the test of God!

What test have you recently completed that you can celebrate because you graduated?

_____

_____

_____

What test is God taking you through now?

_____

_____

_____

What test do you see as possible in your next stage in life?

_____

_____

_____

_____

_____

_____

_____

_____

_____

_____

_____

HE HEARS

Original date: 05/04/2005

Passage: II Chronicles 7:14

[14]if My people, who are called by my name, will humble themselves and pray and seek my face and turn from their wicked ways, then will I hear from heaven and will forgive their sin and will heal their land.

Confession time! There was a time when one of my co-workers was really testing my patience. He was the financial guy, so understandably he wanted every "i" dotted and every "t" crossed. Now that sort of personality is tough to deal with, but as I said, it's understandable. He had to keep the money straight or else everyone would get angry and point the finger in his direction.

My biggest problem with him was that he didn't seem to hear anything I said. For example, we would agree that something needed to be taken care of and we'd even agree on a time. The next day I would get a note from him, asking for the thing we had just agreed on. I would, in turn, either tell him or write him a note reminding him of the fact that we'd already agreed on the specifics and a timeline for the task (which was not one day). Not surprisingly, but much to my frustration, he would turn right around and send me a note the next day, asking for the same thing AGAIN. Now, either he didn't hear me, or he was just not listening. One way or another, there was a huge communication problem.

I am so thankful that God does not treat me this way. I can always rest assured that God hears me. I can always rest assured that God is listening. I don't have to stay awake at night wondering if God heard my prayers. He hears!!!

Remind yourself today that He hears.

What are three specific things that you are asking God for today?

_____

_____

_____

HOPE DEFERRED

Original date: 09/14/2005

Passage: Proverbs: 13:12

¹²Hope deferred makes the heart sick, but a longing fulfilled is a tree of life.

I have no doubt that we were each affected, whether directly or indirectly, by the tragedy caused by Hurricane Katrina. To see the images and hear the stories is like living in a nightmare...hoping...praying that we will wake up and it will all be over. It is unreal!

I personally had an opportunity to volunteer at a shelter in San Antonio, Texas. Imagine never having used a computer but being told that you can "register online" to receive aid or find family members. Imagine not being able to read but being given a sheet with written instructions on how to set up voicemail and then being sent on your way to do it. Imagine having to shower in a port-a-potty outside a warehouse with hundreds of people walking by. Imagine sleeping on a cot two feet away from a total stranger. Imagine spending three hours trying to call FEMA only to get the message, "Due to Hurricane Katrina all agents are busy, please call back later" over and over again.

Working with one man, Mr. Terrance Woods, really opened my eyes like never before. We spent three hours trying to do two things: Mr. Woods needed to register with FEMA, and he was searching the Internet for his displaced brother, Eddie. When Mr. Woods first came over to me, his heart was sick, and it showed. He was distraught. He was frustrated. He felt hopeless. Over the course of those three hours, things began to slowly change for him. We had a very good conversation and by the end, I could see a glimmer of hope in his eyes. Even though neither issue was fully resolved then, he at last felt like he was getting close to a solution.

Speaking with Mr. Woods and being at the shelter made Proverbs 13:12 come alive for me. I saw—firsthand—people with a look of hopelessness on their faces. I saw—firsthand—the sense of utter fulfillment when people finally reconnected with lost family members.

I had to ask myself: What would have happened if there were no phones set up to call loved ones? What would have happened if there was no food at the shelters? What would have happened if clothing was not donated? What would have happened if no one showed up to sort through the donated clothing? What would have happened if all the evacuees were left in the New Orleans Superdome for another 4 or 5 days without food or water? How many more "sick hearts" would we have on our hands?

I ask these questions because I truly believe that one of the main reasons God has blessed me, is so that I can bless someone else. He has blessed me, so that I can fulfill someone's longing, thus helping to reduce the number of "sick hearts" we have in this world.

Why do you feel God has blessed you?

_____

_____

_____

How can you bless someone else?

_____

_____

_____

HOW SECURE ARE YOU?

Original date: 06/29/2005

Passage: Luke 11:21-22 & 24-26 & 20

²¹ When a strong man, fully armed, guards his own house, his possessions are safe. ²² But when someone stronger attacks and overpowers him, he takes away the armor in which the man trusted and divides up the spoils. ²⁴ When an evil[h] spirit comes out of a man; it goes through arid places seeking rest and does not find it. Then it says, 'I will return to the house I left.' ²⁵ When it arrives, it finds the house swept clean and put in order. ²⁶ Then it goes and takes seven other spirits more wicked than itself, and they go in and live there. And the final condition of that man is worse than the first. ²⁰ But if I drive out demons by the finger of God, then the kingdom of God has come to you.

My wife, Jerrilyn, and I had just moved into a new home. With any new move, there is always a lot to consider. You must consider your sleeping arrangements. You must consider your eating arrangements. You must consider your bathroom arrangements. You must also consider your safety arrangements. There's a great deal to set up.

On the issue of safety, we had the locks changed, we covered the windows with curtains, and we even had a security alarm installed.

The security alarm was top of the line. We got all the bells and whistles: Wireless window sensors, touchpad control center, even an extra keypad upstairs!

As the salesman and electricians were walking through the house, we looked to determine which doors and windows needed sensors. We decided that we would only need sensors on the first and second floors as well as in the basement. We figured that the third floor was much too high for anyone to reach. In order to reach the third floor, one would need at least a 40-foot ladder, and who walks around with a 40-foot ladder looking for a house to break into and rob?

One day, as I was walking into our house, something stood out to me as strange. The contractor who built our house was completing two other places next to ours. So, he and his team were there often. Well, I realized that they had been leaving several ladders on the side of the house. These were not just your small everyday ladders. These were 40 and 60-foot ladders. Then it hit me…we had done all we could to protect ourselves and our home and there we were, exposed and susceptible to a break-in.

It made me think about my heart. I often trust in what I think is the right thing to do. I often trust in what I think will protect me. I often trust in my own efforts to protect myself from negative influences. Sure, I can stop talking that way. I can stop watching those shows on television. I can give up this addiction. But are my efforts futile?

No matter how strong I am, all my strength can be overpowered. The only way I can TRULY be delivered and protected from negative influences on my heart is by God. He is the only one who can ensure that tall ladders aren't left on the side of the house, leaving me exposed.

What areas in your life are you relying solely on your own personal ability to protect yourself?

_____

_____

_____

_____

_____

_____

I FORGOT MY JEANS

Original date: 04/12/2005

Passage: Matthew 25: 1-13

¹At that time the kingdom of heaven will be like ten virgins who took their lamps and went out to meet the bridegroom. ²Five of them were foolish and five were wise. ³The foolish ones took their lamps but did not take any oil with them. ⁴The wise, however, took oil in jars along with their lamps. ⁵The bridegroom was a long time in coming, and they all became drowsy and fell asleep. ⁶At midnight the cry rang out: 'Here's the bridegroom! Come out to meet him!' ⁷Then all the virgins woke up and trimmed their lamps. ⁸The foolish ones said to the wise, 'Give us some of your oil; our lamps are going out.' ⁹'No,' they replied, 'there may not be enough for both us and you. Instead, go to those who sell oil and buy some for yourselves.' ¹⁰But while they were on their way to buy the oil, the bridegroom arrived. The virgins who were ready went in with him to the wedding banquet. And the door was shut. ¹¹Later the others also came. 'Sir! Sir!' they said. 'Open the door for us!' ¹²But he replied, 'I tell you the truth, I don't know you.' ¹³Therefore keep watch, because you do not know the day or the hour.

I once had to speak at a banquet held on the University of Connecticut's campus. As I was driving towards the campus, all I saw was open field. It was amazing. I knew that there wasn't much in Connecticut (no offense), but this was truly in the middle of nowhere. There was nothing but cow fields.

Once I arrived on campus and checked into the hotel, a few of the students took me on a tour of their campus. As we were walking around, I mentioned that this place was more country than my hometown, Pine Bluff, Arkansas. They laughed and told me that there are all sorts of animals around campus (UConn was founded as a land grant institution, which I did not know) and that they even had horses to ride.

At this point, I got extremely excited. I had wanted to go horseback riding for over three years now. My opportunity had finally come. I immediately told them to sign me up; I wanted in. As I walked back to the room, bubbling with the joy of an anticipated horseback ride, reality hit me. I had made a huge mistake. I forgot my jeans. I didn't bring anything that was suitable for horseback riding. Had I been wise, I would have done research on their campus and discovered that horseback riding was an option. I missed this wonderful opportunity simply because I was unprepared.

How often do we miss God's blessings because we are unprepared? Next time, let's not forget our jeans.

What is coming up in your life that would benefit from you taking more time to be prepared?

_____

_____

_____

_____

_____

_____

I HAD TO LIE

Original date: 10/12/2005

Passage: Proverbs 16:2

²*All a man's ways seem innocent to him, but motives are weighed by the Lord.*

Jerrilyn and I were dealing with a realtor in North Carolina and noticed that he did something very interesting. We were in the last phase of purchasing a condo in North Carolina. By this point, the realtor we were working with had not done much actual work, but now he was on the case. Our guess is that he was trying to make up for lost time. I completed a final walk-through (the last look you take at a house before the purchase) in the afternoon and noticed that there were several things left undone. One thing was that the water pressure was low. The construction manager (who was on the walk-through with us) said something about being on the third floor and water conservation devices in the faucets causing the water pressure to be low. He said that it was an easy fix and it could be done later.

It was not until we got back to our uncle's house later that evening that we noticed just how low the water pressure really was. We concluded that something had to be done sooner rather than later because the low pressure was simply unacceptable.

Here is where the interesting thing happened. Our realtor called the construction manager and told him, "We returned to the house for a second time that evening and the water pressure was so low that you could not even wash your hands. Only 3-4 drops of water came out of the faucet, and you need to get over there right now to fix it." After the realtor got off the phone, he looked at my uncle and me and said, "I had to lie." It was outrageous…he stood right there and told a bald-faced lie. Some might call it creative liberty, some might call it stretching the truth, some might call it a "white lie," but at the end of the day, a lie is a lie.

The most interesting thing is that he felt like he had to lie in order to get the construction manager to do the job. Because of this, he felt that his lie was innocent. Whether you call it creative liberty or stretching the truth, a lie is a lie. He did not have to lie. All he had to do was simply do his job from the beginning.

After this incident, I had to start asking God to reveal the motives of my heart, because I often think my ways are innocent, when, in reality, they aren't.

When was the last time you felt that you "had to lie"?

_____

_____

In that moment, did you really have to lie? Were there options
that you could have chosen to prevent yourself from being in
that situation in the first place?

_____

_____

_____

_____

_____

LOVE IS MY MISSION

Original date: 11/02/2005

Passage: I Corinthians 13:13

[13] So now faith, hope, and love abide, these three; but the greatest of these is love.

There is nothing like Arkansas home-cooked food. I was reminded of that when my wife, Jerrilyn, and I were in south Arkansas for my aunt's funeral. She was a big fan of cooking and an even bigger fan of eating, so the family made sure there was ample food and we made sure to oblige with ample eating.

At most funerals, people talk about how good the deceased was and how great a life this person led. Most of the time, this is just not true. But for my Aunt Darlene, it was true. Even though the funeral was on a Tuesday afternoon, the auditorium was packed. That's a testament to how much her life touched the lives of so many.

Throughout the entire service, there was a common theme that kept popping up...Love. No matter who you were or where you were in life, Aunt Darlene would always give love. She, herself, was well-educated, earning a master's degree in segregated north Arkansas during the 1950s (a time when that was unheard of). Her education never got in the way of her showing love to others. Story after story was about Aunt Darlene welcoming someone into her home. Story after story was about Aunt Darlene giving her time and money to help out. Her life was about Love. I saw it in those who were there to celebrate her homegoing and I know it personally from how she treated me all my life and how she embraced Jerrilyn.

We were not saddened by her death because while she was here on earth – she lived. Reflecting on her life and our interactions and thinking about the funeral service made me realize something. It made me realize that to live, you have got to love. She loved and her love was limitless. The world was very different because of her love. There were some 500 people in attendance at the funeral and several hundred more who could not make it. Each person was individually touched by her love; each person's life was changed by her love. Love was her mission!

I had to ask myself, how would this world be different if I chose to make love my mission.

Are you willing to make love your mission?

_____

_____

_____

_____

What can you do today to put love into action?

_____

_____

_____

_____

_____

_____

MAKE IT YOUR ROUTINE

Original date: 11/09/2005

Passage: I Thessalonians 5:17

[17]pray without ceasing,

I traveled a lot for one of my previous jobs. There was a time when I was probably home less than a week each month. As a result, when returning home and when preparing to leave for my next trips, there was always a ton to do.

I recall one of the things I had to do – but somehow seemed to keep forgetting – was to put a hold on mail delivery. After telling Jerrilyn about this, she softly suggested that I make it a part of my travel routine.

My first reaction was to get a little upset (internally, of course). I thought to myself, "All the things I have to do and remember to do and she's telling me to add something to my routine...does she not know how busy I am and how much has to get done?" I wondered why she couldn't cut me some slack. I wondered how in the world she expected me to consistently remember that little detail.

Then, I began to think a bit more deeply about what Jerrilyn had suggested. I mean I am blessed with a wife who is wise beyond her years (smile). Suddenly, the benefits of her words became clearer. She was suggesting that I simply "make it my routine" to stop by the post office the day before I left on a trip and complete a hold mail card (this was before you could do it online). It would be like my daily routine of showering or brushing my teeth.

We should take this same attitude towards prayer. Make it routine. Paul tells us to pray without ceasing. He is not talking about falling on our faces, crying, and sweating for three hours, then not praying for three weeks. He is referring to a continuous non-stop commitment to talk to and LISTEN to our Father! He was referring to a routine.

What is your attitude towards making prayer a part of your routine (be honest)?

_____

_____

_____

_____

_____

What changes can you make in your life to make prayer a part
of your routine?

_____

_____

_____

_____

_____

_____

_____

_____

_____

MAKE IT YOUR ROUTINE (PART II)

Original date: 11/16/2005

Passage: Nehemiah 1:1, 3-4, 11

¹The words of Nehemiah....³They said to me, "Those who survived the exile and are back in the province are in great trouble and disgrace. The wall of Jerusalem is broken down, and its gates have been burned with fire." ⁴When I heard these things, I sat down and wept. For some days I mourned and fasted and prayed before the God of heaven....¹¹...Give your servant success today by granting him favor in the presence of this man.

By nature, I'm a problem solver. I always have been. When something goes wrong, my mind jumps to try and figure out a solution. I think about the situation in its entirety. I think about all the players (who is involved or who will be affected by it). I try to develop best and worst-case scenarios and several scenarios in between. I do a little risk-benefit analysis to see which of those scenarios will give the most benefit with the least risk.

I used to think that this was one of the best ways to solve problems. Even though it took a bit of time to reach the optimal solution, it still seemed to work well.

Then, when I was reading Nehemiah, I was thoroughly convicted. Here Nehemiah was, faced with a problem, and the first thing he did was pray. Before trying to develop a solution, before going to someone else for help, before doing anything else, he prayed. In fact, in reading the book of Nehemiah, we find that prayer was a regular part of his problem-solving routine. He would pray and then act.

I have subsequently tried Nehemiah's approach and it has worked wonders. It also helps to prevent me from thinking that I'm the one solving the problem in the first place.

I have decided to make "Nehemiah's problem-solving routine" my problem-solving routine. Pray first, then act (according to God's direction).

Are you more like Nehemiah (pray, then act) or more like I was
(act then pray)?

_____

_____

_____

What are two problems you're trying to solve that you can
pause and pray about before doing anything else?

_____

_____

_____

MAKE IT YOUR ROUTINE (PART III)

Original date: 11/23/2005

Passage: I Timothy 4:13-15

13Until I come, devote yourself to the public reading of Scripture, to preaching and to teaching. 14Do not neglect your gift, which was given you through a prophetic message when the body of elders laid their hands on you. 15Be diligent in these matters; give yourself wholly to them, so that everyone may see your progress.

As a Black man, one of the problems I face is getting razor bumps when I shave. This is not a happy thing. My chin itches. It sometime bleeds, and it just simply does not look or feel good with the itching and irritation. I have tried different types of creams. I have tried electric shavers. I have even tried hot towels. Yet, for some reason, my stubble hair simply decides that no matter what, they are going to curl back into my skin which causes the bumps.

Recently, on a trip home, my father asked me what I was doing for my bumps. I told him that I have tried several things, but not much seemed to work. I also told him that I do not like to use razors because they cause extra bumps. Now admittedly, even though I have tried several things, I was never consistent and diligent in any one method. I would try hot towels for a couple of days, see minor results, but then stop. I would try creams for a couple of weeks, see a few results, but then stop. I was never diligent.

My father told me that an old man suggested using baby lotion as shaving cream. He could not say that it had any medical or scientific merit, but he could say that it worked. So, even though I do not like using razors, I decided to purchase some baby lotion and a new razor and see what would happen. As I was reading the directions on the razor box, I noticed a line that struck me hard. It read, "You must shave consistently for at least 30 days to see results...best results come with consistency." I thought, there it is again. It seems that regardless of the arena you choose, diligence and consistency are the way to see the best results.

Paul told Timothy the same thing. He told him that with diligence (keeping the same routine) in certain areas, progress would come.

Let us be diligent in the things of God. Making them our routine and in turn, seeing great progress.

What are three areas in your life that could use greater consistency and routine?

_____

_____

_____

What barriers keep you from having a consistent routine in those areas?

_____

_____

_____

What three things can you do today to change and take steps towards a consistent routine?

_____

_____

_____

NO ANSWER

Original date: 11/30/2005

Passage: II Timothy 2:15

15Study to shew thyself approved unto God, a workman that needeth not to be ashamed, rightly dividing the word of truth.

As a scientist, I often encounter individuals whose lives are engulfed with answering questions. It is wonderful to see their excitement as they approach various issues, challenges, and problems. However, it is not wonderful when they attempt to use the same scientific approaches and methods to explain (or explain away) God and what He has done. I also encounter individuals of various faith traditions and belief systems. Here too, it is interesting to see them try to explain (or again – explain away) God.

To that end, I once received a wonderful email from a friend of mine who was a professor at Carnegie Mellon University. This friend is a very faithful believer. In his email, he included a list of 7 questions that cannot be concisely answered by any world belief system. If you know of any system, anything, or anyone that can answer these questions (other than the Word of God), please share. Here is his email:

I have composed some questions that I think would bring every human source to the end of itself. Without the Bible, I (the author) cannot even articulate the answers without entangling myself in words.

I don't think any human or belief system can answer them concisely. Recently, two of my Indian students were telling me about their Hinduism and Buddhism beliefs and how it is wonderful because they don't have one source (e.g., the Bible) for all their knowledge. To me, this implies that there is one true and sovereign God who could compose a single book that covers "everything in, before, and after life" in detail in less pages than a dictionary, encyclopedia, or a physics textbook.

Subsequently, I very gently asked them 3 or 4 of these questions (impromptu) and they came to the end of themselves with 3 straight "I don't know" replies. I think this would happen for anybody, including a Christian, who would dare to answer them without using the Bible as his/her answer guide. I did end our conversation by explaining who Jesus Christ is. Only the Bible stands ready to concisely answer questions above human intellect.

7 Questions: No Human or Human Belief System Can Answer These Questions Concisely

1.) How did human life begin? (in 10 words or less)
2.) Is there ever an end for all human life, and if so, how will it occur? (in 10 words or less)
3.) How can I achieve peace in my work, family, and life? (in 10 words or less)
4.) What is the meaning of life (in 15 words or less)?
5.) Ultimate stat: 100% of people die. After death, is there a Heaven or Hell?
6.) If there is a Heaven or Hell, what "exactly" must I do to go to Heaven? (in 15 words or less)?
7.) "Exactly" how many good works must I do to get into heaven?
    (in 15 words or less)?

(ALTERNATE): If answered "NO" to #5, HERE is an alternate #6
*6.) Why do humans die?

SWEET TEA – NO ICE PLEASE

Original date: 07/24/2002

Passage: 2 Timothy 3:5

⁵having a form of godliness but denying its power. Have nothing to do with such people.

I love sweet tea. If you are from the south like me, then sweet tea means SWEET tea (one step away from syrup). When I first got to Boston for graduate school, I did not think I could get real sweet tea. In the south, you can get real sweet tea anywhere, even at McDonalds. Then, I stumbled upon a hole-in-the-wall restaurant called The Silver Slipper (I discovered their sweet tea before I discovered Chef Lee's sweet tea). I actually did not "stumble upon it:" multiple friends took me there. "Stumbling upon it" sounds more exciting.

Sweet tea at The Silver Slipper is made to perfection. You can just imagine grandma in the back brewing and singing hymns. In fact, there was an actual grandma stirring gallons of it daily.

There is one issue though. They started to fill the cups with ice, then pour the tea. They did this without asking if you wanted ice. You order tea and they just fill it up with ice...all the way to the top. This issue has major problems associated with it. First off, instead of 20 ounces of tea (the size of the cup), I only get 8 ounces. The rest is ice...soon to be water. Which is another major problem. The ice turns to water and overly dilutes the tea. Who wants overly diluted tea? Not me! If I wanted watered-down tea, I'd go to any restaurant in downtown Boston.

I totally understood why they add all that ice -- since ice is much cheaper, they could make much more money by giving me less tea. Instead of giving me 20 ounces, they give me 8 ounces and keep the other 12 ounces for the next customer. I get it but what they did not do was reduce the price. So, I ended up with 12 ounces less than what I paid for.

Once I realized this, I had to make a change. So, whenever I ordered tea, I would ask for "sweet tea, no ice." Otherwise, I didn't get as much tea as I could, and my tea eventually tasted watery. But when I asked for "sweet tea, no ice," I'd get a full 12 ounces of grandma's tea.

All too often, we allow our pastors and biblical teachers to "over-ice" the Word. What we get as a result is a diluted mess...no correction, no conviction, no accountability...just a watered-down version of what God wants us to hear.

Are you getting pure sweet tea from your pastors and ministers or are you getting a watered-down mess?

_____

_____

What can you do to ask for "sweet tea, no ice" from those who are there to minister to you?

_____

_____

_____

What can you do to better serve yourself "sweet tea, no ice?"

_____

_____

ONE LAST CONDITION

Original date: 10/05/2005

Passage: John 3:16

16For God so loved the world that He gave His only begotten Son, that whosoever believeth on Him should not perish, but have eternal life.

I remember when Jerrilyn and I closed on the purchase of our first home. It was a complex process. For the weeks leading up to the closing, there is demand after demand to be met. Every other day, we were asked to fax some other document to the lender: bank statements, picture identification, job verification, tax documents, W-2s, and the list goes on and on.

It was absolutely amazing the number of requirements that needed to be met in order to be cleared for closing. Even up to the day before we were supposed to close, I got a phone call from the lender, and they told me that they had "one last condition" that needed to be met before we could be "clear to close". All Jerrilyn and I wanted to do was get through our requirements and start our lives in our new home. Talk about being on edge!

Their requirements and never-ending paperwork were all to determine if I was ready – worthy – to be a homeowner.

Thankfully, God does not require us to provide any paperwork or documentation. He does not need us to justify that we will be able to carry the load of a mortgage. He's not waiting for us to send proof of who we really are. He does not need us to be "ready" for salvation. Often, we think that we need to get ourselves "ready," we think that we need to do one or two more things to be better candidates. Not true. There is only one requirement that we must meet to start our new lives in our new home. All we must do is believe that we are sinners and that His Son died and rose again, so that we could have eternal life.

Have you been trying to fulfill *One Last Condition* before fully turning over the keys to God?

_____

_____

_____

In what ways are you trying to justify yourself to God and how can you turn over the keys?

_____

_____

_____

ONE LAST CONDITION

PILOT STRIKE

Original date: 12/07/2005

Passage: Numbers 23:19

19God is not a man, that he should lie, nor a son of man, that he should change his mind. Does He speak and then not act? Does He promise and not fulfill?

One winter, there was a real possibility of a Delta pilot strike during Christmas. It had me a bit concerned. I understand that pilots must take drastic measures for their own needs to be met. I understand that this sort of thing happens all the time. However, for me, this Christmas was a very bad time for a strike (not that there is ever a good time).

I had a plane ticket, on Delta, to fly to North Carolina on Dec. 23rd. Having not seen my wife for about three weeks, I knew I would be extremely upset if there were no flights.

I realized that I needed to figure out a plan B. I thought through the possibilities: would I book a ticket on another airline? Should I purchase a train ticket? I did not want to be caught unprepared. I mapped out a plan B, but it would take a miracle from God to get me there. God performed the miracle I needed.

This stressful time highlighted the fact that I could not depend on human beings. No matter how much we want to, we cannot do it. We cannot depend on humans – no matter how badly we want to. It's a life lesson that hit home that Christmas. The beauty is that we can always depend on God. He will never let us down. If God says something, you can stake your life on it. God will always come through. There is no need for a plan B, and that was very reassuring.

Has depending on human beings caused you extra, unnecessary stress recently?

_____

_____

_____

What are two things that you can turn over to God and not stress about?

_____

_____

_____

PILOT

STRIKE

SEE IT…HEAR IT…IN IT

Original date: 09/28/2005

Passage: Matthew 16:1-3

¹The Pharisees and Sadducees came to Jesus and tested him by asking him to show them a sign from heaven. He replied, "When evening comes, you say, 'It will be fair weather, for the sky is red,' ³and in the morning, 'Today it will be stormy, for the sky is red and overcast.' You know how to interpret the appearance of the sky, but you cannot interpret the signs of the times".

One afternoon while Jerrilyn and I were at home watching television, we heard news of an impending storm. This was going to be a big one!

As the evening progressed, we began seeing the lightning and hearing the thunder. We sat there listening and watching, then I did something interesting. Something that Jerrilyn thought was very strange. Something that she said was very "country." I looked out the window, saw the lightning, and began saying, "One-one thousand, two-one thousand, three-one thousand, four-one thousand…fifteen-one thousand." Then a loud crash of thunder came. I looked at Jerrilyn and confidently said, "This storm is about 15 miles away." She looked at me like I had lost my mind. Sure enough, 15 minutes later, the storm arrived.

So, I had to remind Jerrilyn that when I was a child, my family would determine how far away a storm was based on the number of seconds between seeing lightning and hearing thunder. Each second meant that the storm was roughly one mile away. It's a phenomenal thing. Well, it proved to Jerrilyn, once again, that she married a country boy.

I thought about that storm and realized that God had designed nature such that if I only paid close attention, I would know how far away a storm was and could adequately prepare. It's simple: each time I would see the storm, then hear the storm, then be in the storm.

If only we paid closer attention to the sight of the lightning and the sound of the thunder, we'd likely be more prepared for the storm WHEN it arrives.

How does God inform you of pending storms?

_____

_____

_____

What do you do when you get signals of a pending storm?

_____

_____

_____

How can you hone your "storm watcher" skills?

_____

_____

_____

Day 22

SMOOTH WALKER

Original date: 06/01/2005

Passage: Psalm 15

¹LORD, who may dwell in your sanctuary? Who may live on your holy hill? ²He whose walk is blameless and who does what is righteous, who speaks the truth from his heart ³and has no slander on his tongue, who does his neighbor no wrong and casts no slur on his fellowman, ⁴who despises a vile man but honors those who fear the LORD, who keeps his oath even when it hurts, ⁵who lends his money without usury and does not accept a bribe against the innocent. He who does these things will never be shaken.

One of the things I pride myself on is walking. I know that might sound strange, but I've always had the ability to walk very long distances at a fast pace without getting tired. More importantly, my walk is smooth. Not to the point that I look like an old charmer in platform shoes, but just enough to exude class, confidence, and clarity of purpose. Some may argue differently, but I like to think it's smooth.

Unfortunately, over the past few weeks, my knees had started to bother me. The knee has four ligaments holding it in place, one at each side to stop the bones from sliding sideways and two crossing over in the middle to stop the bones from sliding forwards and backwards. It is the latter two in the middle that are called the cruciate ligaments, the posterior (meaning back) cruciate ligament and the anterior cruciate ligament (meaning front).

While in high school I had to have reconstructive surgery on my anterior cruciate ligament (ACL). Since then, I've been in a constant state of rehabilitation. Part of rehabilitation is to exercise my leg muscles. The muscles in my leg act to keep the bones in my knee bones from touching. This is particularly important to me since I no longer have my original ACL, and thus my knee bones are more likely to rub against each other causing extreme pain. So, stronger leg muscles mean less knee pain. The pain really becomes a problem after walking for extended periods of time.

I've rarely experienced the pain when I've exercised regularly, and it has never affected my smooth walk. That is, until I stopped working out. There was a period of time when work had me so busy that I wasn't able to get into the gym. As a result, I started to experience extreme pain in my knee. This pain really affected my walk. It was not to the point where I had a noticeable limp; however, the pain kept me from having the smooth walk I once had.

It's amazing how not exercising one part of my body (my legs) caused pain in another part (my knees) and essentially destroyed my smooth walk.

All of this made me wonder how my spiritual walk was affected by a lack of exercise in my spiritual life. I wondered if lack of spiritual exercise (prayer, Bible study, and obedience to God) caused a limp that is noticed by others.

Have you neglected spiritual exercise just long enough for you to feel the pain but it was not noticeable to others? When?

_____

_____

Have you neglected exercise so long that others can now see your spiritual limp?

_____

_____

What can you do today to restart (or start) your spiritual exercise routine?

_____

_____

STRONG STOMACH REQUIRED

Original date: 05/11/2005

Passage: Romans 12:1-2

[1] Therefore, I urge you, brothers, in view of God's mercy, to offer your bodies as living sacrifices, holy and pleasing to God—this is your spiritual act of worship. [2] Do not conform any longer to the pattern of this world but be transformed by the renewing of your mind. Then you will be able to test and approve what God's will is—his good, pleasing and perfect will.

While I was assistant dean at MIT, we would have monthly staff meetings where we would usually have an icebreaker to open the meeting. In one meeting, the icebreaker was to tell about your worst food experience. It was hilarious to hear these different stories.

I told about a time when I had curry chicken at a church function. My stomach was bubbling over for two days after eating that chicken. The chicken tasted pretty good, but the effect on my stomach was as if someone put demonic poison in it. It was so bad that the musician (who shall remain nameless) couldn't make it through an entire song without going to the restroom.

One of the other staff members told a very interesting story about a time that her family visited China. On this visit, they were in a small remote village having dinner with a very poor family. She said that it was obvious that this family had put a lot of energy, effort, and money into this meal. They prepared a meal that, in the village culture, was considered a dinner for special occasions. During the meal, they brought out what was considered the ultimate delicacy (a very expensive course). The delicacy was 1-2-day-old baby birds! I kid you not. She said that they had little baby birds in a bowl, and they were eating them like popcorn. Now the real kicker is that these 1-2-day-old birds were alive and moving. Nonetheless, the family ate them like popcorn.

To keep from insulting the family, she said she ate one of the little (living) baby birds. She did it to please the family! That seemed "extremely extreme" to me. But then I thought, how far are we willing to go to please God?

Are you willing to do the thing that seems strange if it means God is pleased? Have you done it before?

_____

_____

_____

_____

THE DAY A DAY WENT AWAY

Original date: 05/18/2005

Passage: Matthew 25:13

[13] "Therefore keep watch, because you do not know the day or the hour.

One day I, along with my beautiful wife, were unpacking boxes in our new home in Boston. Anyone who has ever moved knows the level of time and energy required to settle. At this particular time, I happened to be two weeks from the beginning of a 10-week summer program that I managed. This would be my first time ever running a summer program, and of course it was going to host a class 4 times the size of any previous class. There was a seemingly insurmountable mountain of details that needed to be addressed. However, the reason things had piled up was my own procrastination.

Knowing that I also needed to head to DC that week for a conference and thinking to myself, "This is a horrible time to travel", I laid out an elaborate plan to try and catch up on overdue things. The plan was structured so that I'd be able to essentially accomplish 5 days of work in 3 days (I was to leave for DC on a Thursday). It went something like this:

Monday

☐	Purchase airline tickets
☐	Call faculty mentors
☐	Drop car off at auto shop
☐	Contact summer interns
☐	Update summer program website
☐	Purchase supplies at Home Depot
☐	Attend thesis defense
☐	Meet with other MIT summer program managers
☐	Finalize summer calendar, request health forms from students

Tuesday

☐	Security system set-up (11am-3pm)
☐	Wash clothes
☐	Contact remaining faculty mentors
☐	Purchase items at Target
☐	Management team meeting
☐	Complete student evaluations
☐	Fax financial papers
☐	Pick up mail at post office
☐	Organize financial accounts for summer program
☐	Get haircut
☐	Clean house for Jerrilyn's weekend guests

	Wednesday
	Delivery of final furniture (10am – 1pm)
	Pack clothes
	Send snack attack
	Confirm summer program speakers
	Drop boxes of books off at PR firm
	Purchase supplies at Home Depot
	Hang blinds and pictures
	Change flight time
	Have lunch with students at Media and Technology Charter HS

I think you get the point by now. There was obviously a lot more to do than I had time for. I was going to try with all my heart to get everything done because it was all very important. I should mention again that most of these things had been on my list for a couple of weeks and could/should have been completed sometime before I reached this point.

Then a crazy thing happened to me. Monday went well and I completed just about everything on my list. I knew that I was not going to leave until Thursday afternoon, so it was looking pretty good in terms of catching up on things. I went into the office on Tuesday morning feeling good. Then I had a conversation with my boss. She asked if I was packed and ready for the trip. I told her that I was not but was going to get a haircut today (Tuesday) and pack tomorrow (Wednesday). She looked at me strangely and asked if I was sure I would have enough time to pack, since we were leaving tomorrow (Wednesday). I laughed and responded, "You might be leaving on Wednesday, but I'm not leaving until Thursday." After looking at our travel records, I discovered that SHE WAS CORRECT! I was thinking, "How in the world could I have missed that?" More importantly, how was I going to get caught up on things?

Essentially, I had lost an entire day! This would not have been much of a problem if I had been more prepared and taken care of things earlier. Procrastination had gotten the best of me! At this point, several things simply could not get done.

Then I thought, how often do days slip away in my spiritual life? How often are there things within the ministry that God wants me to do, that I must forfeit due to my own procrastination? If God said, "Today is the day, let's go," would I be ready?

Are there things you've been putting off that you should go ahead and knock out? What are they?

_____

_____

_____

If God said "Okay, let's go", would you be ready? Why or why not?

_____

_____

_____

_____

_____

_____

TURNED TO STONE

Original date: 04/27/2005

Passage: Hebrews 3:12-14

12 See to it, brothers, that none of you has a sinful, unbelieving heart that turns away from the living God. 13But encourage one another daily, as long as it is called Today, so that none of you may be hardened by sin's deceitfulness. 14We have come to share in Christ if we hold firmly till the end the confidence we had at first.

I remember when I made the dreaded visit to see my dentist. It had been a while since my last visit, so I knew things would not be promising for me. I had convinced myself that the reason for delaying my visit was due to being extremely busy, but it was more because I didn't want to hear about how bad my teeth were.

After waiting for a short time (completing forms and getting x-rays taken), the dentist finally called me to the back. She took one look at my teeth and said, "You don't floss do you?" After verbally thrashing me for my tooth negligence, she explained what happens when I don't floss. When tiny food particles are caught in the teeth, they get compressed and begin to harden. Over time, these tiny particles stack on top of each other, are compressed more, and harden more. They eventually create a layer of stone over my teeth. To remove the stone, she had to drill and pick and pull for almost an hour. Now that was painful!

Sin does the same thing in our lives. Tiny sins that go unchecked will compress and harden around our hearts. It also creates a layer of stone that keeps God out and destroys us. The solution...floss every day. Read God's Word and allow Him to reveal tiny sins to us. Once revealed, repent of those tiny sins so they won't harden our hearts.

How can you take time to spiritual floss each day?

_____

_____

_____

_____

Are there sins that have hardened and turned to stone? If so, are you willing to do what it takes to remove the stone?

_____

_____

_____

TURNED TO STONE

VIKI

Original date: 05 / 25 / 2005

Passage: Proverbs 3:5-6

⁵Trust in the LORD with all thine heart; and lean not unto thine own understanding. ⁶In all thy ways acknowledge him, and he shall direct thy paths.

While on Christmas break one year, Jerrilyn and I rented an SUV and drove to visit our family in Virginia. We chose an SUV because we wanted to be very comfortable on that long drive. The one we received was "top-of-the-line." It had all the latest gadgets, including a navigation system. This was our first time in a car with a navigation system, so we were quite excited (Okay, maybe it was just me who was excited). This navigation system was so tight that it spoke to you and told you which way to turn (yep, I'm dating myself). Since it was a woman's voice, we named her "Viki" (after the main computer in the movie *iRobot* with Will Smith).

The way a navigation system works is as follows. Imagine that the earth is a grid where each location corresponds to a spot on the grid. The navigation system in your car has a device that sends a signal to a satellite in space. The satellite then knows where you are on the grid, and it also knows where most other places on earth are on the grid. Where you are is like "point A" and where you want to go is like "point B". The navigation system can then determine the shortest path to get you from "A to B". Clearly, this was WAY before the proliferation of GPS/navigation systems because now we all have them on our phones.

Once Jerrilyn and I were all packed up, we jumped in the SUV and told Viki that we wanted to go to Virginia. She determined the shortest path for us, and we were off!

Anyone who has traveled long distances knows that you never follow your original path exactly. There are all sorts of pit stops (food, restroom, shopping, etc.). You also know that, even with a map, you can get lost. Well, whenever we would make a turn that was not along the shortest path, whenever we "got lost," Viki would promptly tell us, "You are off the pre-determined route, please follow the new path."

What was happening was that each time we got off the path, Viki (knowing where we needed to go) determined a new path for us based on where we were. This made me think: Wouldn't it be nice to have a Viki for our life path? Wouldn't it be nice to know that if I made a wrong turn in life, a new path to my destination would be determined? Wouldn't it be nice to know that I did not have to remain lost?

Then it slapped me in the face...we already have that...it's the Bible!

Do you feel off your path in life?

_____

_____

_____

If so, what are three things you can do to tap into your spiritual Viki?

_____

_____

_____

WHAT YOU DO REALLY
MATTERS!

Original date: 10/19/2005

Passage: Philippians 1:27, Proverbs. 20:11

²⁷ Whatever happens, conduct yourselves in a manner worthy of the gospel of Christ

¹¹Even a child is known by his actions, by whether his conduct is pure and right.

I am a huge fan of movies. I love action movies, like *The Matrix*. I love dramas, like *Lean on Me* or *E.T.* I even enjoy love stories, like *Love & Basketball*. I just love movies.

To me, there is something about watching a person take on the role of a character and really become the part. It is amazing. In fact, there are actors that I adore, simply because I adore the characters they play. There are also actors that I totally despise, simply because I despise their characters. There is also something about watching a plot unfold. From the set-up to the climax to the resolution, I love it all.

However, there is a trend in movies. If you begin to watch closely, you'll notice it. In most movies, the main characters (good and bad) do things that are immoral and inexcusable. Unfortunately, the movie typically leaves this part unaddressed. They settle for resolution of the big issue and ignore dealing with the immoral and inexcusable acts of individuals. It's as if they are almost saying to us, "Who cares about what you do, it does not really matter." "The end justifies the means."

This could not be further from the truth. What we do DOES matter. Both in our personal and professional lives, it matters.

Both Paul and Solomon admonish us to watch what we do because it matters. Let's not be like those in the movies. Let's live according to a higher standard. What you do really does matter.

If you were a character in a movie, would someone look at you and say, "They have unresolved immorality and it's inexcusable"? Why or why not?

_____

_____

_____

_____

_____

_____

THEY TOLD ME
I HAD A WINDOW SEAT

Original date: 04/06/2005

Passage: Numbers 23:19

19God is not a man, that he should lie, nor a son of man, that he should change his mind. Does he speak and then not act? Does he promise and not fulfill?

There I was, sitting on the plane and minding my own business. I was reading Barack Obama's book, waiting for the plane to take off, and missing my beautiful wife. Just when I thought everyone was on the plane, in walks this lady who had a strange look on her face. It was the sort of look that lets you know something was about to go down.

She was supposed to sit two rows ahead of me. On my side of the plane there was an aisle seat, a middle seat, and a window seat in each row. In her row, a nice young couple occupied the window and the aisle seats.

As she approached the row, she looked at the seats, then she looked at her ticket, then she looked at her seat, then she looked at her ticket again. Suddenly, she said, (in a very aggressive voice I might add), "They told me I had a window seat."

After examining her ticket, she acknowledged that based on what her ticket said, she had an aisle seat, but she would not let go of the fact that the ticket agent told her she had a window seat. She simply had to have a window seat. She stood there and would not move until she got her window seat.

After about three or four minutes of her repeating, "They told me I had a window seat," the nice young couple gave in and moved over. She finally had her window seat.

What was telling to me was that she was willing to stand and wait (despite holding up the plane) for what she recalled. Forget the fact that someone was in the seat, forget the fact that the paperwork said something else, and forget the fact that she was keeping a plane from taking off. She held strong to her recollection. To her it was a promise.

What if we were the same with God's promises?

How willing are you to stand on God's promises even when the tangible evidence points to something different?

_____

_____

_____

_____

_____

How willing are you, like the young couple, to move over so that someone else can have a seat (even when they are rude)?

_____

_____

_____

_____

WORLDWIDE CERTIFIED

Original date: 10/26/2005

Passage: II Timothy 2:15

*15Study to shew thyself approved unto God, a workman that need not to be
ashamed, rightly dividing the word of truth.*

Early in our marriage, Jerrilyn was on active duty with the
United States Air Force. When she was in her last week of
a two-month course in San Antonio, she had to spend that entire
week "in the field." They also call it ambush training.

Being "in the field" meant that she, along with her unit,
would live in the field, find their own food, make their own fire,
sleep on the ground, navigate by compass, and a host of other
"outdoors" type things. If you know my wife, then you know that
she is not the outdoors type. This was a very interesting week for
her.

The unit even got ambushed (hence the name) by Marines
who were hiding in the field. The purpose of the ambush was so
the unit could train to be ready for any challenge it would face in
combat. The unit was training because it is pretty much a given
that the enemy would attack at some point.

The United States Air Force has decided to invest tremendous resources towards training its soldiers to be ready for almost any situation. They must be ready to survive in the city, in the field, or in the jungle. They take classes and undergo training and are fully expected to execute the things that are learned. They are fully expected (and properly trained) to be Worldwide Certified. In other words, they can go anywhere in the world and fulfill missions set forth by the United States Air Force.

All this training that Jerrilyn had to undergo had me thinking and asking several questions.

As Christians, how certified are we? Are we prepared for an enemy ambush? Can we go anywhere and defend the gospel? Or better yet, what number of resources are our Christian leaders investing in our preparation? Are they helping us to be Worldwide Certified or are we simply City Certified? Are we even City Certified? Are we, ourselves, making the effort to be Worldwide Certified?

What one thing can you do today to be more Worldwide Certified?

_____

_____

_____

What one person can you help, this week, to become more Worldwide Certified?

_____

_____

_____

Day 30

WHERE'S YOUR LADDER LEANING?

Original date: 12/19/2003

Passage: Proverbs 3:5

⁵Trust in the Lord with all thy Heart and lean not unto thy own understanding.

One of the most quoted scriptures is Proverbs 3:5-which says, "Trust in the Lord with all thy heart and lean not unto thy own understanding." That scripture is great. When things look confusing or life becomes difficult, we quote that scripture. When people ask us how to make challenging decisions, we quote that scripture. But do we really know what it means to trust in the Lord? I have always believed that we work our way up a ladder of understanding and that ladder is either leaning on our house (our own understanding) or faith (trusting in the Lord). I thought I leaned on faith until I began to experience the scripture more deeply while my wife was deployed to Afghanistan.

My wife, Jerrilyn, had been deployed to Afghanistan during her time with the United States Air Force. We prayed with all our might that she would not have to go, but she had to go. It was somewhat devastating. Our understanding could not make sense of it at the time. So, we were in a position where we HAD to trust that God knew exactly what He was doing. We had to figure out how to continue to trust at a moment we had no clue what was going on. We didn't know to trust that things were just going to work. The way people quote this scripture, it should be easy to just trust. But it was not.

One thing is for sure, though; during tough times like these, all you can do is stand still and know that He is God. We stood still. We didn't make any decisions. We didn't try and push any agenda. We just stood and waited on God. We believed that one day, He might reveal His ultimate plan; but even if He didn't and even if we didn't understand, we were going to lean on Him and not our own understanding. For us that meant surrendering, and not forcing an outcome.

God eventually made it crystal clear why He allowed her to be deployed when He did, and it was a tremendous blessing.